Message

Having a Credit Card these days isn't just about convenience. It is an important and necessary part of our daily lives. Leveraging on Credit Card facilities makes managing payments easier. But it is also a big responsibility.

Along with the convenience and rewards, there are many fees, charges and payments that come with Credit Cards. Credit Cards presence may be widespread, the proper knowledge and understanding of Credit Cards and how to use them is quite rare.

With our publication "Using Credit Cards: Smartly, Wisely, Prudently" we aim to reach all users of banking credit facilities and provide knowledge that is relevant and beneficial. The more you know about Credit Cards, the more likely you will be to use this powerful tool wisely.

We hope you find the information in this book useful.

For more, visit www.LearningPrudence.com

Using Credit Cards

- *Smartly*
- *Wisely*
- *Prudently*

CONTENTS

- 01   Message
- 05   Credit Card Quiz
- 11   Introduction: What is a Credit Card?
- 14   Pros And Cons of Credit Cards
- 15   Important Terms To Know
- 19   Common Fees And Charges
- 23   Credit Card Statement - What To See
- 27   Credit Limit
- 29   Making Minimum Payments
- 33   Reward Points
- 37   Worst Mistakes You Can Make With Your Credit Card
- 41   Good Habits of Responsible Credit Card Users
- 45   In Summary
- 47   Credit Card Info Checklist
- 48   Yes or No?

All right reserved © 2013 Learning Prudence

Published in Singapore by Learning Prudence

Email: contactus@learningprudence.com

First Edition 2013

Author: Rajdeep Ghai

Graphic Designer: Leo

ISBN-13-978-1-4935-6904-5

No part of this publication may be reproduced, stored in a retrieval system or transmitted in any form or by any means, electronic, mechanical, photocopying, recording or otherwise, without prior permission from the publisher.

Credit Card Quiz

*Answer each of the following questions honestly. Mark your answers to all the questions and then score your results. An honest assessment will help you understand your own gaps in knowledge. Good Luck!!!
The answers are at the end of the quiz.*

CREDIT CARD QUIZ

Each questions has one correct answer

Q1. What is a Credit Card?
- ☐ (a) A loan agreement that allows you to spend now and pay back later
- ☐ (b) Money to buy things you would normally not be able to buy immediately
- ☐ (c) Free use of someone else's money
- ☐ (d) A means to enjoy life now and pay in future.

Q2. What is the main advantage of using a credit card?
- ☐ (a) It makes it easy to buy because you can always pay later
- ☐ (b) It doesn't cost anything to use
- ☐ (c) It is convenient because you don't have to carry cash
- ☐ (d) You can afford to buy things that normally you would not be able to.

Q3. What do you think is a prudent percentage of ones monthly income that should be used for paying credit card bills?
- ☐ (a) 0% - 15%
- ☐ (b) 16 % - 30%
- ☐ (c) 31% - 50%
- ☐ (d) More than 50%

Q4. When paying your credit card bill, what must you do?
- ☐ (a) Pay at least the total minimum payment and be sure it is received by the payment due date.
- ☐ (b) Drop it in the mail the day it is due
- ☐ (c) Skip it this month if you've got a lot of other bills
- ☐ (d) Don't worry about the due date since you're paying online

Q5. What does APR stand for?
- ☐ (a) Advanced Promised Rate
- ☐ (b) Adjustable Percentage Rate
- ☐ (c) Annual Percentage Rate
- ☐ (d) Actual Paid Rate

Credit Card Quiz

Q6.	**If you carry a balance of $5,000 in credit card debt, you don't make any more charges and pay only the minimum payment due each month of $100, how long will it take to pay that balance off if your card provider charges an interest of 23.99%.**
☐	(a) 8 years
☐	(b) 16 years
☐	(c) 24 years
☐	(d) Over 30 years
Q7.	**Jane got a credit card offer with a low introductory rate. What does she need to find out before she accepts the offer?**
☐	(a) How long the low rate will last?
☐	(b) What the rate will be after the introductory period ends?
☐	(c) What are the fees associated with the offer?
☐	(d) All of the above
Q8.	**Credit card issuers always give you a "grace period" to pay for your purchases before finance charges are applied.** ☐ True ☐ False
Q9.	**Studies have shown that people spend more when they are using credit cards than when they are shopping with cash.** ☐ True ☐ False
Q10.	**Before applying for a credit card, the most important question to ask is:**
☐	(a) What are the fees, charges and other fine print that come with this card?
☐	(b) What are the free gifts and other offers that this card comes with?
☐	(c) Do I really need extra credit limit?
☐	(d) How does this card compare to other credit cards?
Q11.	**Which of the folowing are signs that debt may be a problem for you?**
☐	(a) You have maxed out the credit limits on your credit cards
☐	(b) You have had to skip paying some of your bills, or you've paid some late
☐	(c) Bill collectors have started calling
☐	(d) All of the above

Q12. Which of the folowing will be a right method of calculating monthly interest charge on your credit card?
- ☐ (a) The APR, multiplied by your balance
- ☐ (b) APR divided by 12, multiplied by your average balance
- ☐ (c) APR multiplied by your new charges
- ☐ (d) APR multiplied by the balance unpaid from the previous month

Q13. Do you check your statements for all charges every month to ensure that there are no erroneous charges.
☐ Yes ☐ No

Q14. Do you pay your monthly balance in full and do not roll over your payments?
- ☐ (a) Always
- ☐ (b) Most of the times I pay in full. If I am not able to, I pay back as quickly as possible. Normally I don't roll over my payments
- ☐ (c) I always pay the minimum outstanding amount for my card each time and I never miss that.
- ☐ (d) I try to pay the minimum outstanding each time but sometimes I miss that payment also.

Q15. What does an introductory 0% APR credit card mean?
- ☐ (a) The 0% APR is the interest rate on a credit card for a fixed period of specified time
- ☐ (b) A temporary interest rate on a credit card for a specific period of time, later adjusted to a higher interest rate
- ☐ (c) An interest rate available only for new customers which stays at a 0% APR for the entire life of the credit card
- ☐ (d) None of the above

Q16. This month you have to pay $500 by the due date on your credit card. You pay only $400. In the next months statement, you will be charged interest only on the $100 left outstanding ($500 due - $400 paid)
☐ True ☐ False

Credit Card Quiz

Q17. *The interest rate charged on a credit card is higher than:*
The interest rate charged on a personal loan + A standard mortgage rate

☐ True   ☐ False

Q18. *Your credit card gives you 28 day grace period between a charge on your card and the payment due date. Last month you could not pay the full outstanding amount. This month you spend $2,000. You will get the 28 day grace period before interest is charged on this new purchase.*

☐ True   ☐ False

Q19. *Which of the following is true for credit cards offering an interest free balance transfer?*

☐ (a) They will charge you a much higher rate on new purchases than your old credit card provider
☐ (b) The interest rate at the end of the interest free period will be significantly higher than that on your old card
☐ (c) The repayment made each month will in the first instance clear the interest free balance, leaving the interest and new interest accruing balance untouched
☐ (d) All of the above

Q20. *If you owe $1,000 on card A at 10% APR and $10,000 on card B at 15% APR and have $1,000 to pay off some of your debt, what is the best choice?*

☐ (a) Pay off card A
☐ (b) Decrease your card B balance
☐ (c) Pay $500 to card A and $500 to card B
☐ (d) Pay $300 to card A and $700 to card B

CREDIT CARD QUIZ

Answers

Q1. a	Q11. d		
Q2. c	Q12. b		
Q3. b	Q13. Yes		
Q4. a	Q14. a		
Q5. c	Q15. b		
Q6. d	Q16. False		
Q7. d	Q17. True		
Q8. False	Q18. False		
Q9. True	Q19. d		
Q10. c	Q20. b		

Score Table

Give yourself 1 mark for every correct answer. Add up all your marks to get your total score.

If your total score is:

<10   Destroy your credit cards before they destroy you.

11-15   You need to learn a lot about credit cards.

16-19   Well done! Don't lose your trick and continue to be on top.

20   Would you like to join us?

Introduction
What is a Credit Card?

The card may feel like plastic but it is money. Just because a credit card does not look, smell or feel like real money, does not mean it is any different from cash.

What is a Credit Card?

When you buy something with cash, you pay for it immediately. When you pay using a credit card, generally you pay later, but you still have to pay.

In a nutshell, a credit card is just a different way of paying.

How you pay back your credit card outstanding balance, defines what a credit card is to you.

Credit card is a loan. If you pay back on time it can be an interest free loan. If you pay later, it can be a very expensive loan.

Paying with a credit card is same as paying using real money.

5 girls bought the same red dress costing $250. But they all ended up paying different amounts for the dress.

Fiona, Michelle, Joyce, Angel, Stephanie

How is it possible that for the same dress, same price, they pay different amount? The answer lies in how they use their credit cards.

What is a Credit Card?

Michelle paid for the dress using her credit card. She did not spend beyond her credit limit. She did not use her card for cash advance. When Michelle got her statement, she paid the balance in full. The dress cost her

Stephanie paid for the dress using her credit card. When she got her bill, she paid only the minimum payment and kept paying minimum amount due till she paid the full amount. She did not use the card for anything else. The dress cost her **$425**

$250

Angel already had an outstanding amount from her last statement. When she got her next statement, she kept paying the minimum till she paid for her dress. By purchasing the dress, she also went beyond her credit limit. The dress cost her

$631

Fiona used a brand new credit card with 0% introductory APR. But she took a cash advance that raised her APR to 23.99%. She forgot to make payments many times and paid only the minimum due every month. The dress cost her

Joyce did not have any outstanding on her card. When she got her bill, she paid more than the minimum required each month, but could not pay the full outstanding amount each time. The dress cost her **$347**

$811.50

Guide To Using Credit Cards ~ Smartly • Wisely • Prudently

Pros and Cons of Credit Cards

Pros

* It is convenient to carry a card instead of carrying cash.

* Some credit cards offer warranty coverage for purchases along with the option to dispute and block the charges, in case of a problem.

* For certain types of transactions, only credit cards are usable (example, purchases over the internet) and for certain types of transactions, using cash is antiquated (example car rentals, hotel room deposits).

* When travelling, it is easier and less risky to carry a credit card rather than bundles of notes (although travelers checks are also safe and convenient).

* A good credit history through timely payments helps you get cheaper loans.

Cons

* It is easy to spend more on credit cards. Actually it is too easy to spend more using credit cards.

* Once the credit card payments get out of hand, it can be very hard to regain control.

* The interest rate on credit card loans is exorbitantly high.

* There are too many traps and several fees and charges, example minimum payment trap, late fees, over the limit fees, bounced check fees etc.

Important Terms To Know

Master the vocabulary of credit cards.

Important Terms To Know

ACCOUNT NUMBER / CREDIT CARD NUMBER
This is a unique number assigned to a credit card. On a credit card, this number is embossed on the face of the plastic.

ANNUAL FEE
An annual (yearly) fee associated with having a credit card. This is normally a flat amount and does not depend on interest rate.

ANNUAL PERCENTAGE RATE (APR)
The yearly percentage rate charged when a balance is held on a credit card. This rate is applied each month on the outstanding balance on the credit card.

AVERAGE DAILY BALANCE
This is the method by which most credit cards calculate your payment due. An average daily balance is determined by adding each day's balance and then dividing that total by the number of days in the billing cycle.

Important Terms To Know

BILLING CYCLE
The time between billing statements. Generally it is about 1 month but can vary.

OUTSTANDING AMOUNT
This is the balance amount to be paid after the due date. APR is applied on this amount plus a late fee charge.

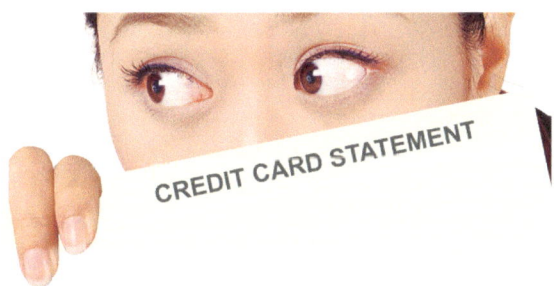

BILLING STATEMENT
A written record prepared by a financial institution, sent usually once a month, listing all transactions for the account, all fees and other charges, and the interest being charged.

CASH BACK CARDS
Cash back cards returns to you a percentage of the total amount spent on your credit card over a specific period of time. This feature is particularly useful if you normally pay your credit card bills in full each month, as it gives you an effective discount on the products bought with your credit card.

CREDIT LIMIT

This is the maximum allowable credit that you can use on your credit card. A lot of cards do not allow you to spend beyond this limit. A few cards however let you spend beyond it but charge you a higher rate of interest (APR) and a fee associated with it.

GRACE PERIOD

A period of time during which you are allowed to pay your credit card bill without being charged a finance charge and/or late fee.

INTRODUCTORY RATE

A temporary, lower annual percentage rate, that is raised after a period of time

PRE-APPROVED CARD

Unfortunately this doesn't mean much. It is basically a marketing ploy to coax you to apply for another credit card. A credit card offer with "pre-approved" only means that you as a potential customer have passed a preliminary credit check. A credit card company can still deny a customer it invited with "pre-approved" card once the actual application is received.

Common Fees and Charges

*The real cost of privilege,
points and free gifts.*

Common Fees and Charges

ANNUAL FEE
An yearly fee charged for the privilege of having a credit card (Really?!?) Normally it is charged once a year. Most banks now offer some cards with no annual fees but most of their promotions, discounts and deals are only applicable on cards that have annual fees. A lot of times, the primary card may not have annual fees, but the "FREE" supplementary card that comes with it has an annual fee.

HOW TO AVOID IT:
Prevent it. There are a lot of credit cards that don't charge any annual fees. Find them and use them.

LATE FEE
A charge for making less than the minimum payment by the due date on your statement. All cards charge this and can be charged in every billing cycle. This charge is added to the outstanding amount on your credit card.

HOW TO AVOID IT:
Prevent it. Always make your payments on time or before. If possible, put automatic payments from your account to the credit card company on the due date.

INTEREST FEE/ FINANCE CHARGE
This is the monthly interest charge for not paying your outstanding amount in full and carrying the credit card balance to the next payment cycle. All cards have it unless they are in their 'introductory 0% interest rate' period which will have several terms and conditions around it. The actual rate of interest depends on the card type but just know that it is a very high rate of interest.

HOW TO AVOID IT:
Prevent it. This is irresponsible use of money and should be prevented at all costs. Don't just make minimum payments, pay the full outstanding every time.

Common Fees and Charges

CASH ADVANCE FEE

This is a charge for taking advance or borrowing cash on your credit card. Most cards charge this and generally there is no interest free grace period for this kind of an advance. Each time you make a cash advance, this charge will hit you.

HOW TO AVOID IT:
Stay away from it. Avoid cash advances on your credit card. Use an ATM if needed.

OVER-THE-LIMIT FEE

This is a fee charged to your account if your spending goes above your credit limit. A lot of banks don't charge it, but then a lot of banks do.

HOW TO AVOID IT:
Don't touch it with a barge pole. Keep your spending within the credit limit.

RETURN CHEQUE FEE

This fee is charged if you make a payment by cheque and the cheque is returned/bounced because of insufficient funds in your account. All cards issuers will charge this fees.

HOW TO AVOID IT:
Prevent it. Ensure you have sufficient funds. If possible, put automatic payments from your account to the credit card company on the due date.

BALANCE TRANSFER FEE

This fee is charged when you transfer a balance from one card to another. A lot of cards offer no balance transfer fees facility or no interest charges for balance transfer but these are all short term teaser rates and have several conditions attached to them.

HOW TO AVOID IT:
Avoid it. Best way is to keep paying your credit card bills so you don't accumulate enough that you need to transfer around. In the case you do need it, research all details, terms and conditions before deciding which balance transfer offer to take.

Credit Card Statements
~ What To See

The basic information that you MUST see in every statement.

Credit Card Statements
~ What To See

1

TOTAL OUTSTANDING AMOUNT
How much do you owe your credit card company.

 *This is the amount that you have to pay. And ideally you should pay back the full amount.*

2

DUE DATE
By when do you need to pay this amount. Make a note of this.

 *This is the date by which the payment must be received by your credit card provider. Not the date by which you send the cheque.*

3

MINIMUM AMOUNT DUE
This is what you have to pay to avoid late charges. This is not what you owe. This is not what you should pay. Pay the full amount due or as much of it as possible.

 *Not paying this will incur late fees. Just paying this will incur massive interest charge on the balanced unpaid amount. Check "Calculator" section on www.learningprudence.com for the impact of minimum payment.*

Credit Card Statements ~ What To See

TRANSACTION DETAILS
Go through your transactions to understand your total outstanding amount

 ***Boring? Difficult? Complicated?
Roll up your sleeves and spend 10 minutes going through the details of your statement.***

Unpaid from last statement	How much is it? Did you pay late?	How was the interest calculated?

+ New Transactions − Payments Made − Credits

Any reversal of charges, any other amounts that should be added to your account?

 ***Go through it carefully. Make sure you did spend on the things that are on your statement.***

ANY CHANGES IN TERMS AND CONDITIONS
Any changes to the:
- Billing cycle/ dates/ grace period
- APR (Interest Rate)
- Fees and Charges

 If there are any changes, update the credit card information template at the end of this book.

**Normally people don't go through their statements and just make a payment.
Going through your statement in details:**
1. Ensures you are not getting hit by erroneous fees and charges.
2. If you are missing payments, making them late, rolling them over, then seeing it again and again on your statement will force you to take action and not hide behind the excuse of being busy.
3. Most importantly, once you are more aware of what charges you put on your card, how much you buy and what you buy, you will be less impulsive and more in control of your spending.

Guide To Using Credit Cards ~ Smartly • Wisely • Prudently

Credit Limit

*Spending limits do not make you rich.
It is only a reflection of how much
you CAN spend not how much
you SHOULD spend.*

Credit Limit

My credit limit is $15,000.

That's nothing, my credit limit is $25,000.

You people live in kid's land. I stay where you seperate men from boys. My total limits are $50,000.

I am a power woman. I can buy what I want. My banks have given me a spending limit of $75,000.

My spending limits are only $8,000.

- *Spending limits do not make you rich. It is only a reflection of how much you **CAN** spend not how much you **SHOULD** spend.*
- *Spending should be need / reason based and in line with your income and repayment capability.*
- *Spending limit should be based on how much you need to manage your expenses comfortably. Not on how much banks want to give you. Banks would like you to spend more. That's how they will make money.*
- *Remember - Whatever you spend, you have to pay back. And more.*

Making Minimum Payments:

The HIGH cost of LOW payments

My credit card statement says my outstanding amount is $1,300. There is an option to pay only $65.00. Isn't that great? The minimum payment is so affordable.

The HIGH cost of LOW payments

CREDIT CARD STATEMENT

Account Number: 5674-1234-1234-0001

Past Due Amount	Outstanding Amount	Minimum Amount Due	Due Date
$2800.00	$5000.00	$100.00	07/09/13

John has an outstanding credit card debt of *$5000* and his credit card company charges an interest rate of *23.99%* per annum. Unfortunately, he does not have any money now. So he decides to just pay the minimum amount due, which is *$100*. He does not expect any windfall of money soon, so he thinks he will continue paying *$100* every month till he pays back his full outstanding.

In how much time you think John will be able to pay back his outstanding credit card debt? *50 months? 8 years? 10 years?*

In reality, it will take John *32 years* and *7 months* to pay back the full amount. And in this time, he will pay the bank a total of astounding *$39,320.*

That is the danger of Minimum Payment. It seems so easy to make a minimum payment as it gives you a <u>false sense of security</u> of having handled your credit card payment. In reality <u>you have just fed a monster.</u> Card users think everything is "fine" with their credit as long as minimum payments are being made. In reality, though, they could be taking on more debt than they can afford.

Making Minimum Payments : The HIGH cost of LOW payments

ILLUSTRATION: Suppose you buy a computer and pay the minimum amount every month. How much will the computer end up costing you?

Computer

CALCULATING THE REAL COST
Your purchase:

A Computer cost **$2200**

You pay per month **$100**
Time taken to pay off: **30 months**
Total cost approximately **$2928**

*APR (Annual Premium Rate) = 23.99%

IN THAT MUCH AMOUNT YOU COULD HAVE BOUGHT:

Computer ($2200) + A Printer ($300)

+ One pair of sneakers ($50) + 20 lunches at a fastfood ($160)

+ Six T-shirts ($100) + Two pairs of Denim ($100) = **And still have some money left**

If you know that a computer will cost you 30% more than the advertised price, you will probably never purchase it. But by purchasing it on credit card and making minimum payments, that is what you end up doing.

Guide To Using Credit Cards ~ Smartly • Wisely • Prudently

Minimum payments end up extending your obligations for a very long time. It may even happen that making minimum payments also becomes difficult. The problem to tackle is to eliminate the debt. Not prolong it. Use credit card as a convenience. Not as a financing option.

Conversely, the more you pay each month, the faster you eliminate this debt. In the example of John, what if John decides to pay $200 every month instead of $100. How much time will it take to pay back the $5000 and how much will he pay in total? He will be able to pay back his card debt in 3 years !!! And he will pay a total of $7000.

The table below shows you how the amount you pay affects the duration of your pain and the amount of interest you have to pay.

Credit Card Outstanding: $10,000 Interest Rate: 23.99% per annum		
Note: Assuming that there is no new charges on the credit card		
Payment Per Month	Time to Pay off Debt	Total Interest Paid
$200	32 Years 10 Months	$68640
$250	6 Years 10 Months	$10305
$500	2 Years 3 Months	$2889
$1000	1 Year	$1264

How much does it cost you? Really.

The other important effect of minimum payment is that as you stretch your payments, the costs of your purchases increase many folds over time.

Reward Points

Wow! My card rewards me? Isn't that great?

Is it really a "reward" if you are paying for it? Chasing credit card rewards is generally speaking, a losing game.

Reward Points

In most cases, the value of a point would be between 1-3 cents.

Think: *Why is your bank incentivizing you to spend more money? What's in it for you?? What's in it for them???*

Congratulations! You have 62.5 million dollar point on your card.

62.5 million, Wow! We are rich! what can we buy with these dollar points?

Go to Las Vegas!

Get a Ferrari!

If you put in extra $100, you can redeem a Spa Package!

Learning Prudence

Reward Points : Wow! My card rewards me? Isn't that great?

The Fine Print On Reward

① **There are limits on how much reward you can get.** Many credit card companies offer a large percentage of cash back (5% cash back on purchases) but reveal in small print that it is up to a maximum amount of cash back you can get, certain types of expense are not included and there may even be a minimum spend that you have to do to qualify for the reward.

② **Blackout dates:** Not every spend may go towards rewards. Some companies block out dates on which the spend will not be counted. For example Christmas spends may not be counted towards rewards. Also there are blackout dates for redemption. For example, if you want to redeem airlines miles, you may not be able to do it over holidays (which makes it difficult to utilise them).

③ **Like all good things, they expire.** If you don't get to actually use your rewards, then you don't really benefit from the rewards. A lot of cards have expiry dates and banks don't want to remind you of the expiry. After all, It will cost them money.

④ **Teaser Rewards** - 0% APR! 10,000 miles!! Free tickets!!! These are good rewards but the fine print has many catches - does it apply to all types of expenses? Is it for a fixed period or ongoing? Is there a window in which you must redeem them? You must make sure to read all details before assuming that the reward is a given.

5 **Annual Fee Waiver -** *This is probably the most common reward. The main catches are: It may be only for the first year, it will not be applicable for supplementary cards even though you have an auto application for it and there might be a minimum spend associated with getting this reward.*

6 **Not applicable everywhere -** *Some cards offer double reward points, triple reward points and more, but these are applicable to certain stores only. And a lot of card companies do not count internet transactions as a spend towards reward points.*

7 **You pay for your redemption -** *this is the biggest killer. You 'earn rewards'. But when it comes to taking the benefit of those, then you are charged for redemption. A lot of people miss noticing it, but several card companies charge these amounts in the regular statement where it goes unnoticed.*

8 **Value of rewards points.** *Cash back credit cards are quite straightforward to evaluate. But when card companies give you points as rewards, then they are very difficult to assess the value of. You know that you get 1 point per dollar spent. What is the point really worth? To know whether or not you're getting a good deal, you need to take the time to understand how the points relate to $ values.*

The WORST MISTAKES you can make with your Credit Card

WORST MISTAKES

① **Making Minimum payments**
It takes years to pay back and makes billions for banks. **THIS IS BY FAR THE WORST THING YOU CAN DO.**

② **Not paying your outstanding in full**
Credit card debt is extremely expensive. **NOT WORTH IT.**

③ **Taking Cash Advances**
Cash advances do not have interest free period and they incur fees also. **USE ATM OR USE RESTRAINT.**

④ **Falling for Teaser Rates**
Every Credit Card offer will expire. Understand the charges on the card after the introductory period expires. **USE PRUDENCE.**

⑤ **Playing Balance Transfer Game**
Credit Card companies provide wonderful offers for free Balance Transfers. They all have a promotional rate, they expect you to make a mistake in that period so the rate can go up sooner and on top of it, there is usually a balance transfer fee. Focus on reducing your balance, not shifting it around. **AVOID THIS TRAP.**

The Worst Mistakes you can make with your Credit Card

Paying Annual Fees
Credit Cards are not a status symbol. There are several credit cards available that are free for life. **PAYING ANNUAL FEES IS A NO NO.**

Not paying credit card bills on time
This is plain and simple throwing good money after bad. Never ever pay late. Pay a week in advance if needed. **PAYING LATE FEES IS IRRESPONSIBLE USE OF MONEY.**

Spending for Rewards
The value of rewards is usually not worth the price you pay for them – either directly as fees or indirectly as higher spending. **YOUR GREATEST REWARD IS YOUR MONEY SAVED.**

Putting Daily Expenses on Credit Cards
One golden rule is: If you are going to consume it within the next two days, use cash. You will be in control of your spending that way.

Another rule can be, if it costs less than $20, don't use your credit card. Usually we spend a little bit more because it is on credit. That's why they have a lot of impulse purchase things just next to the check out cashiers line. **THERE IS NOTHING WRONG IN RESPONSIBLE USAGE OF CARDS.**

Exceeding your credit limit
This just incurs unnecessary over-the-limit charges. **WORST THING YOU CAN DO IS TO TAKE ANOTHER CARD. BEST YOU CAN DO IS TO CONTROL YOUR EXPENSES.**

Not reading the fine print
There is a reason why the fine print is so small, runs into so many pages and is confusing to read. Because they don't want you to read the fine print. **THAT IS WHERE ALL THE DANGERS LURK. READ FINE PRINT TO AVOID TO FALLING INTO UNNECCESSARY TRAPS.**

Taking up Retail Credit Cards
They are a great deal on the one time purchase and the ongoing discounts. But they are all counting on you to spend more money because you have their card. And the more cards you carry, higher the chance that you will make a mistake that will cost you more than all the discounts you have aggregated. **AVOID RETAIL CREDIT CARDS.**

Buying things you don't need. We all are guilty of this –
buying things we don't need because they are on credit. If you reflect back on your statements, you will be surprised at things you bought that you didn't need to. Another golden rule: If any thing costs more than $200, wait a couple of days before buying it and then go back to the store if you still really need it. **BE A JUDICIOUS SPENDER.**

Having Too Many Cards
If you apply for a card just because the commercial or the poster appeals to you, you are likely to have a huge stack of cards in your wallet. This just increases the likelihood that a payment slips through the cracks . You basically need only 3 cards:
**1 GENERAL PURPOSE CARD FOR DAILY PURCHASES
1 FOR MILES OR ANY OTHER REWARDS
1 WITH HIGHER LIMIT FOR RARE BIG PURCHASES.**

Good Habits of Responsible Credit Card Users

Good Habits of Responsible Credit Card Users

 They pay off credit cards in full every month.

 They know that credit cards encourage overspending because we become casual with what we buy when we don't see cash going out of our pockets.

 They stay within 30% of their credit limit on every card.

 They minimize the number of cards in the wallet. (Why increase temptation?)

 They track their credit card expenses regularly and properly. They don't throw away receipts and card slips till they compare the spends to statements.

 They read their credit card disclosures and other terms. It is difficult but 20 minutes reading those can save you a lot of time and pain later.

Good Habits of Responsible Credit Card Users

 *They don't use credit cards for day-to-day and casual purchases. They always carry sufficient cash for such expenses. IF IT COSTS LESS THAN $20, THEY USE CASH!*

 *They never use credit cards to buy things they cannot afford.*

 *They don't fall for cheap advertising tricks and don't take every card that comes their way.*

 *Most importantly, they know that CREDIT CARDS are MONEY. A card is not FREE Cash. WHAT YOU SPEND, YOU HAVE TO PAY BACK. AND THE LATER YOU PAY, THE MORE YOU HAVE TO PAY.*

In Summary

Non-Prudent Use of Credit Cards

Credit cards can provide instant gratification. You want something right now, but don't have the money, you can pay using a credit card and pay back later. You feel powerful. You feel in control. You can spend as you like.

It doesn't strike you immediately, but you still have to pay for it. Because you are not seeing money go in front of your eyes, the reward of the purchase is not linked to the cost of purchase.

And pretty soon from being in control of your money to satisfy your desires, the payments control you and what you are able to do with your money.

BIGGEST PROBLEM WITH CREDIT CARD PURCHASES IS:

 Buying things *YOU CANNOT AFFORD*

 Buying things *YOU DON'T NEED*

 Buying things *YOU DON'T NEED NOW*

 Buying things *BECAUSE THEY ARE ON A "GREAT DEAL"*

And all this is enabled by paying just with a swipe of the card. All the things that look affordable are only things you can pay for, not what you should pay for.

Credit Card Info Checklist

Credit Card Info Checklist

Fill this up for every credit card you have. Ask the bank staff for information if needed.
Download this template for free from www.LearningPrudence.com

Date: .... **Bank/ Lender Name:** ....

Credit Card Type (Visa/ MasterCard/ American Express Etc.): ....

Credit Card Number: ☐☐☐☐ ☐☐☐☐ ☐☐☐☐ ☐☐☐☐

- On what date of the month is the monthly cycle closed and the bill generated?
  .... (dd)
  (If it is a double cycle card, meaning bills come twice a month, then put both the dates)

  Is it the regular payment date: ☐ Fixed / ☐ Variable

	Year 1	Year 2	Year 3	Year 4	Year 5
■ What are the annual fees on the card?					
■ What are the annual fees on supplementary cards?					
■ Is there a minimum spend I need to do to waive the annual fees					
■ How many points are needed to offset against annual fees?					

■ How long is the interest free period: • If you paid the last outstanding balance in full ? • If you did not pay the last outstanding balance in full ?	.... days .... days
■ What is the regular APR	.... %
■ Is the APR	☐ Fixed ☐ Variable ☐ Tiered
■ If you make late payment, does the APR go up because of that?	☐ Yes ☐ No
■ How much is the late fee?	$ ....
■ Do you allow transactions that go beyond credit limit to go through or do you reject them?	Approved/Rejected
■ What is the fees for going over the approved credit limit	$ ....
■ What % of outstanding is the minimum payment that you need to make every month?	.... % or $ ....
■ What is the charge for cash advance?	$ ....
■ Do cash advances have an interest free period?	☐ Yes ☐ No
■ Due date for payments from you to the bank is (a or b)	a) When the payment is received by the bank? b) When the payment is credited to your card account?
■ What is the approximate value of 1 reward point	.... cents

Guide To Using Credit Cards ~ Smartly • Wisely • Prudently

Yes or No?

So are Credit Cards good or bad? Answer is, It depends on you!

They are a useful tool. And like any other tool, its usefulness depends on how you use it. Fire is a tool. It can be used to cook food and keep warm. And it can burn down houses and forests if not used carefully.

Important thing is to know yourself and be smart about your cards. Using any tool smartly requires you to be trained in using it. And that is what you need: An education in using credit cards and a proper maintenance and care of how you use your credit cards.

Can't credit cards be used responsibly? Yes. And a lot of people do use them responsibly. But it is not an easy thing to do. It requires a lot of tender loving care in how you spend, how you pay and how you manage your cards.

www.ingramcontent.com/pod-product-compliance
Lightning Source LLC
Chambersburg PA
CBHW040922180526
45159CB00002BA/574